THE COMMANDANT

THE COMMANDANT

A MONOLOGUE

THE RUDOLF HOESS TEXT
EDITED BY JÜRG AMANN

AFTERWORD BY IAN BURUMA

Overlook Duckworth

New York • London

This edition first published in hardcover the United States and the U.K.
in 2012 by Overlook Duckworth, Peter Mayer Publishers, Inc.

NEW YORK
141 Wooster Street
New York, NY 10012
www.overlookpress.com
For bulk and special sales, please contact sales@overlookny.com

LONDON
90-93 Cowcross Street
London EC1M 6BF
inquiries@duckworth-publishers.co.uk
www.ducknet.co.uk

First published in Germany in 2011 by Arche Verlag

The Rudolf Hoess text is excerpted from material translated
into English by Andrew Pollinger and previously
published under the title *Death Dealer* by Promethus Books

Cataloging-in-Publication Data is available from the Library of Congress.

A catalogue record for this book is available from the British Library.

Manufactured in the United States of America

Book design and type formatting by Bernard Schleifer

ISBN: 978-1-59020-677-5 US
ISBN: 978-0-715-64162-0 UK

1 3 5 7 9 10 8 6 4 2

"Since my arrest, my handcuffs
have not been opened."

—*Rudolf Hoess*

EDITOR'S NOTE

Jürg Amann

IN THE FACE OF REALITY, all fiction is obscene. Especially in cases in which reality is accessible, even if it is denied repeatedly. Perhaps then more than ever. I have never felt this truth so powerfully as when *The Kindly Ones* by Jonathan Littell was published a few years ago—a novel that effectively empathizes with a fictional Nazi officer.

Around the same time, while doing some theater work in Vienna on a similar theme, I happened upon the writings of Rudolf Hoess, the commandant of Auschwitz. There, I found what I was looking for. From this personal testimony, this terrifyingly naïve self-denunciation, I found a deeper and more affective truth than any fiction could present.

Hoess wrote his thoughts down cold—without the slightest trace of remorse or even comprehension—while awaiting trial in Krakow, between his arrest at the end of the war by British military police and his death sentence by the highest state court in Poland. The result was a document that stretched over three hundred tightly printed pages.

Here, I have distilled their essence into a monologue in sixteen parts. Nothing is invented. Scarcely a word has been added or a sentence changed, and, when it has, only for reasons of composition or for better comprehension. Here, in these pages, is the life of Rudolf Hoess in his own damning words. Originally conceived for the stage and as a radio play, perhaps this original monologue can now have its effect as a read drama as well.

I

I, Rudolf Hoess, SS Kommandant at Auschwitz, will try in the following pages to write about my deepest personal thoughts and feelings. I will attempt to recall, to the best of my memory, all the important events, all the highs and lows of my psychological life, and the experiences which affected me. For the reader to completely understand the entire picture I will sketch, I must return to my earliest child-hood memories.

My family lived in an average home outside of Baden-Baden until I was six. In the surrounding area there were only isolated farmhouses. I had no playmates at all, because all the children in the neighborhood were older. I was often lured into the nearby Black Forest by the tall pine trees. Most of the time, however, I went to the stables to see the horses. If someone wanted to find me, all he had to do was to go to the stables. I was absolutely fascinated by horses. Even the wildest bull the farmer had was my best friend. I was never afraid of dogs, and they never harmed me either. My mother tried everything to break me of this obsessive love of animals, but it was completely useless. I was and would always be a loner. I had an irresistible passion for water. I had to constantly wash and bathe. I would take any opportunity to wash or bathe in a tub or stream that flowed through our garden.

When I was six years old, we moved to the Mannheim area, which was outside the city, but to my deepest regret there were no stables and no livestock. My mother often reminisced how for weeks on end I was heartsick for my animals and my forest. On my seventh birthday, I was given Hans, a coalblack pony with flashing eyes and a long mane. I was exploding with joy. I had finally found my friend. In the area where we now lived there were playmates my age. With the few friends I had, I played the same childish games and all the pranks as children have throughout the ages all over the world. But best of all, I enjoyed going with Hans into the Haardt Forest, where we were all alone, riding for hours on end without a living soul around.

Life became more serious once school started. I studied hard, did my homework as quickly as possible, so that I could have time to play around with Hans.

My parents gave me the freedom to do as I wanted because my father had made a vow that I would lead a religious life and become a priest. The way I was raised was entirely affected by this. I was raised in a strong military fashion because of my father. Because of his faith, there was a heavy religious atmosphere in our family. My father was a fanatic Catholic. I especially liked his stories about his services in East Africa: his descriptions of the battles with the rebellious natives, their culture and work, and their mysterious religious worship. I listened in radiant rapture as he spoke of the blessed and civilizing activities of the missionary society. I resolved that I would become a missionary no matter what, and that I would go into darkest Africa, even venture into the center of the primeval forest. It was especially exciting when one of the old, bearded African fathers who knew my father in East Africa came to visit. As time allowed he would take me on pilgrimages to the holy places of our country, yes, even to the hermitages in Switzerland and Our Lady of Lourdes in France. He fervently prayed for heaven's blessing so I would become an inspired priest. I myself believed deeply, as much as one can as a child, and I took my religious duties seriously. I prayed with the proper childish reverence and was zealous as an altar boy.

Even from childhood on up, I was trained in a complete awareness of duty. Attention to duty was greatly respected in my parents' home, so that all orders would be performed exactly and conscientiously. Each person always had certain responsibilities. My father paid special attention to see that I obeyed all his orders and instructions, which were to be carried out painfully. I can still remember a time when he got me out of bed because I left the saddle blanket hanging in the garden instead of in the barn where he told me to hang it to dry out.

A warm relationship existed between my parents, full of love, full of respect and mutual understanding. And yet, I never saw them being affectionate to one another. But at the same time, it was very seldom that they exchanged an angry or bad word between them. My two younger sisters were four and six years old. They were around my mother a great deal and loved to cuddle with her, but I refused any open show of affection, even from my early years on, much to the constant regret of my mother and all of my aunts and relatives. A handshake and a few brief words of thanks were the most that one could expect from me. Although both of my parents cared for me very much, I could never find a way to confide in them. I would never share any problems, either big or small, which occasionally depress young people. Inwardly I struggled with all these things by myself. The only one I confided in was my Hans. He understood me, as far as I was concerned. My two sisters were very attached to me and tried repeatedly to form a good, loving relationship with me. But I never wanted to bother with them. They always remained strangers to me.

I respected and admired my parents very much, my father as well as my mother. However, love, the kind of love which I came to know later as a parent, I could not pretend to show for them. Why was this? I cannot explain, and even today I can find no reason.

I was never what you would call a good boy, or even an ideal child. I played all the pranks which a young mind in those years could invent. I ran with other boys through the wildest games and fights or whatever came along. I always was able to get my way. If someone did something wrong to me, I did not rest until I felt I had gotten even. I was relentless and I was feared by my classmates. Oddly enough, I sat at the same desk during my whole time in high school with a Swedish girl who wanted to become a doctor. During all the years of struggle in school, we understood each other like good buddies, and we never fought.

You should know that I took my religion very seriously. The first serious crack in my religious belief happened when I was thirteen years old. On a Saturday morning, during the usual pushing and shoving to be the first one into the gym, I accidentally pushed a class-mate down the stairs. Throughout the years, hundreds of students must have sailed down these stairs without any serious injuries. This time he was unlucky; he broke his ankle. I was punished with two hours of detention. I went to confession in the afternoon as I did every week, confessed what I did like a good boy, but I didn't say anything about this incident at home because I didn't want to spoil Sunday for my parents. They would learn about it soon enough during the coming week. That evening my confessor, who was a good friend of my father, was visiting at our house. The next morning my father scolded me about the pushing incident, and I was punished because I did not report it to him right away. I was devastated, not because of the punishment, but because of this unheard-of breach of confidence by my confessor. My faith in the holy profession of the priesthood was smashed and doubts began to stir within me. The deep, true, childlike faith which so calmly and surely guided my soul until this time was smashed. The following year my father died suddenly.

World War I began. I constantly nagged my mother to let me volunteer to help at the Red Cross. I can still see the blood-soaked head and arm bandages, the uniforms smeared with blood and dirt, our grey prewar uniforms, and the blue French uniforms with the red trousers. I can still hear the suppressed moaning during the loading of the wounded into the hastily requisitioned streetcars, as I ran among them passing out refreshments, cigarettes, and tobacco. After school I was always in the military hospital, the barracks, or the railroad station watching the passing troop transports or hospital trains and passing out food or gift packages. In the hospitals I saw the seriously wounded as they quietly moaned to themselves. I always crept timidly past those beds. I saw the dying and the dead. A strange feeling shuddered through me, but I can't describe this accurately anymore. These sad pictures were quickly erased by the humor of the lightly wounded or those who had no pain. I never tired of listening to their stories of the soldier's life. The soldier within me blossomed. Throughout many generations of my ancestors on my father's side had been officers. In 1870 my grandfather died as a colonel leading his regiment.

I wanted to be a soldier and I didn't want to miss this war. All my thoughts and efforts were directed to becoming a soldier. School, my future, and my home came second. My mother was powerless against my efforts. In 1916, with the help of a captain in the cavalry whom I had met in the hospital, I succeeded in quietly sneaking into the regiment in which my father and grandfather had served. I arrived at the front line after a brief period of training. All this happened without my dear mother knowing. I never saw her again because she died in 1917.

I had many new experiences during our layover in Istanbul, which was still rich in Oriental tradition, and on the horseback ride to the distant Iraqi frontline. And all this before I'd even reached the age of sixteen.

I clearly remember my first firefight with the enemy. Right after we arrived at the front line we were assigned to a Turkish division. Our cavalry unit was divided into three regiments in order to give the Turks some backbone. As we were being assigned, the English [New Zealanders and Indians] attacked. When the shooting got heavy, the Turks ran away. Our small German unit lay alone between the rocks and ancient ruins defending our skins in the vast expanse of desert. Comrade after comrade fell wounded, and the one lying next to me didn't answer my calls. When I turned to look at him, I saw he was bleeding from a large head wound and was already dead. Until then, I had not fired a single shot as I fearfully watched the slowly advancing Indians. I can still picture to this day a tall, broad Indian with a distinct black beard, jumping from a pile of rocks. For a moment I hesitated, the body next to me filling my whole mind, then I pulled myself together even though I was very much shaken. I fired and watched the Indian slump forward during his jump. He didn't move. I really can't say if I aimed correctly. He was my first kill! The spell was broken. Still unsure of myself, I began firing and firing, just as they had taught me in training. During the advance I hesitated and reluctantly looked at my kill. It made me feel a little squeamish. It was so exciting for me that I can't say whether I wounded or killed any more Indians during this first firefight. After the first shot I aimed and shot carefully at those who emerged from cover. My captain mentioned his amazement at how cool I was during this, my first firefight, my baptism of fire.

It was strange for me to have such a great trust in my captain, my soldier father. I worshiped him a great deal. It was a much more intimate relationship than I had with my own father. When he died in the spring of 1918 during the second Battle of the Jordan, I mourned for him with great pain. His death really hit me hard.

In early 1917 our outfit was transferred to the Palestine front in the Holy Land. All the familiar names from religion, from history, and from the legends about the saints came back to me again. And how different it was from the way we had pictured it in our youthful fantasies from descriptions and pictures.

In the hospital at Wilhelma, a young German nurse took care of me. It was at this time that I had my first sexual experience. I had been shot through the knee and also suffered a terrible relapse of malaria that lasted quite long. I needed special care and had to be watched closely, since I caused a great deal of damage during my delirious ravings due to fever. This nurse took care of me so well that my mother couldn't have done better. As time passed I noticed that it wasn't motherly love that caused her to nurse me in such a loving way. This first experience of love, with all its tenderness and affection, became the guideline for the rest of my life. I never again could joke about sex. Sexual intercourse without affection became unthinkable for me. So I was spared from having affairs and from the brothels.

World War I ended. I had matured far beyond my age, both inside and out. The schoolboy who had run away from home and trembled with fear during his first battle had become a rough, tough soldier. At the age of seventeen I was decorated with the Iron Cross and I was the youngest sergeant in the army.

At the time of the armistice, we were in Damascus, Syria. I had definitely made up my mind not to be put in a POW camp under any circumstances. I had decided to fight my way back to the Fatherland by my own power. The Army Corps advised against it. After asking around, all the men of my platoon volunteered to fight their way back with me. Since the spring of 1918 I was leading my own cavalry platoon. All the men were in their thirties; I was only eighteen. Our adventure took us through Anatolia [Turkey]. We sailed on a miserable derelict ship across the Black Sea to Varna and rode on through Bulgaria and Romania. We traveled the deepest snows through the Transylvanian Alps, on through Transylvania, Hungary, Austria, and finally we reached the Homeland. After three months of helplessly wandering about with no maps, using only the geography we learned in school, requisitioning food for men and horses, fighting our way through Romania, which had become our enemy again, we reported to our reserve unit.

Even during the war, I had doubts about my vocation to be a priest. The incident with my confessor and the trade in holy relics that I had seen in the Holy Land had destroyed my faith in priests. I also had many doubts about the Church. Little by little I began to reject the profession my father had always praised, but I didn't consider any other profession. I never spoke to anyone about this. Before my mother died she wrote in her last letter that I should never forget what my father wanted me to be.

After my return, my guardian and all my relatives pestered me to enter a seminary for priesthood so that I could find the right climate to prepare me for my prescribed profession. My uncle wanted to force me to do as my parents had chosen by saying that he would not give me any money to train for any other profession.

Burning with anger, I left my family's home without saying goodbye. The next day I went to East Prussia to sign up with a volunteer outfit destined for the Baltic States. So the problem of my profession was solved; I became a soldier again. I found a home again and a feeling of being sheltered in the camaraderie of my fellow soldiers.

The battles in the Baltic States were more brutal and vicious than anything I had experienced before, during World War I or afterwards in all the battles of the Free Corps. There was hardly a front line; the enemy was everywhere. Wherever the opposing forces collided, there was a slaughter until no one was left. Countless times I saw the horrible pictures of burned-out cottages, the scorched and partially burned bodies of women and children. When I saw this, I could not believe that the mad desire of humans to destroy could be intensified. At that time I could still pray, and I did.

Since the government had to deny the existence of the Free Corps, it could not prosecute or investigate crimes such as theft of arms, espionage or treason committed by members of these organizations. A kind of self-justice system based on historical German patterns came into existence within the Free Corps and their offspring organizations. These were the so-called Vehmic courts. Any kind of betrayal was punished by death. And so many traitors were executed. However, only a few cases became known, and only in a few individual cases were the guilty caught and sentenced by a special federal court called the Protection of the Republic, which was created specifically for this purpose.

In the Parchimer Vehme murder trial I was sentenced to ten years in prison. This is how my trial came about. A group of us had beaten to death a man named Parchimer, who betrayed a friend named Schlageter to the French. I was accused of being the ringleader and main participant. I don't have to empha-size that I agreed with the killing of the traitor. Since in all probability no German court would have sentenced him, we passed judg-ment on him by an unwritten law which we had instituted ourselves because of the need of the times. Very probably only those who have lived through that time themselves, or who can put themselves into that troubled period, can understand.

IV

The bitter awakening came soon, shortly after my transfer to the penitentiary. A new, unknown world opened up for me. Doing time in a Prussian prison was no vacation in those days. Until then I believed I had seen it all as far as people were concerned. The criminals in the penitentiary taught me differently. Even though I sat alone in my cell, I still came into daily contact with other prisoners. Most importantly, I overheard their discussions at the windows during the evening. And those conversations gave me insight about the thinking and psychology of this class of criminals. An abyss opens up to me about human aberration—vices and passions. At the start of my time in prison, one evening I overheard one prisoner in a nearby cell tell another how he robbed a forester's house after making sure that the forester was safely seated in a tavern. During the robbery he killed the maid with an axe, then murdered the wife, who was in her final month of pregnancy. After that he took the four little children, one by one, and smashed each head against the wall until they stopped screaming, because they were crying. He told about this foul deed with such vile and brazen expressions that I would have loved to get at his throat. I could not get to sleep that night. Later on I heard about many more depraved things, but they did not upset me as much as what I had first heard that day.

A good book has always been a good friend to me. The only problem was that up to now because of the unrest of the kind of life I led, I had neither time nor leisure for this. In the solitude of my cell it became everything, particularly in the first two years of my imprisonment. It was my recuperation, and with this I could forget my whole situation.

After two years had gone by without anything special happening, suddenly a strange condition came over me. I became very irritable, nervous, and excited. I couldn't stand doing any work. I was a tailor at the time, and I had enjoyed it. However, I was unable to eat. I couldn't read anything anymore and I couldn't concentrate at all. Like a wild animal I paced rapidly back and forth in my cell.

I wanted to pray, but all I could manage was a sad, fearful mumbling. I had forgotten how to pray; I could no longer find the way to God. In that state of mind I believed that God didn't want to help me anymore because I had left him. My officially leaving the Church in 1922 tortured me. And yet, this was only the result of a condition which had existed since the end of the war. Even though it happened gradually, I had already cut the ties to the Church during the last years of the war. I reproached myself bitterly for not having followed the will of my parents, for not becoming a priest. Is it possible to communicate with the dead? In my hours of greatest agitation, before my thoughts became confused, I often saw my parents standing before me in the flesh and I spoke with them as if I were still under their care.

V

After six years I was free again. The gift of life was given back to me!

After my release from prison, I got in touch with the Artamans. I had become acquainted with this organization and its goal during my imprisonment through their writings. This was a community of young patriotic people, young men and women who had come out of the youth movement from all national alignments. They wanted to escape the unhealthy, decaying, and superficial life of the cities, especially the large metropolitan areas. They sought the natural way of life in the country. They abhorred alcohol and nicotine, in fact everything that was not good for the healthy development of mind and body; moreover, through this principle of living they hoped to return to the soil from which their ancestors came forth, to the fountain of life of the German people, to the healthy farming community. This was also my way, my long-sought goal.

In the first days there I became acquainted with my future wife, who, along with her brother, was inspired by the same ideals and had found her way to the Artamans. We knew from the very first moment that we belonged together. We got married as soon as it was possible [in 1929], in order to start our hard life together, a life freely chosen out of deepest inner conviction. Clearly we both saw the long, difficult, and trouble-filled road to our goal, but nothing was going to prevent us from reaching it.

During that time three of our children were born for the new tomorrow, for the new future. Our own land was soon to be allotted to us. But it did not happen that way! Himmler asked me to join the SS in June 1934. This now was to pull me away from our planned path. The temptation to be a soldier again was really strong, much stronger than my wife's doubts about whether this profession would fulfill and satisfy the inner me. She agreed, however, when she saw how very much I felt attracted to becoming a solider again.

When Himmler made the call to join the SS, to enter the guard troop of a concentration camp, I had no thought at all about the concentration camps that were mentioned in the postscript. During the isolation of our farm life in Pomerania, we had hardly heard about concentration camps.

VI

I arrived at Dachau and became a recruit again, with all its joys and sorrows, and then I became a drill instructor.

I remember precisely the first flogging I ever witnessed. According to Inspector of Concentration Camps Eicke's orders, at least one company of troops had to be present at the administration of this punishment. Two prisoners had stolen cigarettes from the canteen and were sentenced to twenty-five blows of the cane. The soldiers lined up in a U-shaped formation with their weapons. The punishment bench stood in the middle. The two prisoners were presented by the block leaders. The Commandant put in his appearance. The camp commander and the senior company commanders reported to him. The duty officer read the sentence and the first prisoner, a small, hardened, lazy man, had to lie down across the bench. Two soldiers from the troop held his head and hands firmly while two block leaders carried out the sentence, alternating after each blow. The prisoner didn't utter a sound. It was different with the second one, a strong, broad-shouldered, political prisoner. After the first blow, he screamed wildly and wanted to tear himself loose. He continued screaming to the last blow, even though the Commandant told him repeatedly to be quiet. I stood in the front rank and I was, therefore, forced to watch the entire procedure in detail.

I say forced because if I would have stood further back, I would not have looked. Hot and cold chills ran through me when the screaming started. In fact the whole procedure, even the first beating, made me shiver. Later, during the first execution at the beginning of the war, I was not as upset as during this corporal punishment. For this I can find no explanation. Why did I shy away from this punishment so much? Even though I try, I cannot explain this.

The block leaders who were so eager to

watch them and whom I really got to know later were almost always two-faced, vulgar, very violent, and vile creatures who behaved the same way toward their fellow soldiers and their families. To them prisoners were not human beings.

I must now admit, I conscientiously and attentively performed my duty to everyone's satisfaction. I didn't let the prisoners get away with anything. I was firm and often hard. But I had been a prisoner for too long for me not to notice their needs. It was not without inner sympathy that I faced all of the occurrences in the camp. Outwardly I was cold, even stone-faced, but inwardly I was moved to the deepest. I saw many crimes, suicides, or those shot while trying to escape. I was close enough to determine if they were real situations or set up by the guards. I viewed the work accidents, those who died by running into the electrified wire. I was present at the legal identification of bodies in the autopsy room, during disciplinary beatings, and during the punishments Commandant Loritz ordered done and often observed himself. These were Loritz's punishment assignments and his way of fulfilling a sentence. By looking at the stone mask on my face he was firmly convinced that he didn't have to "toughen me up," as he loved to do with the SS men who seemed to him to be too weak.

This is when my guilt really begins. It had become clear to me that I was not suited for this kind of service because in my heart I did not agree with the conditions and the practices of the concentration camp as demanded by Eicke. Right then I should have gone to Eicke or Himmler and explained that I was not suited for service in the concentration camp because I had too much compassion for the prisoners. I did not have the courage to do this. I did not want to reveal myself because I didn't want to admit my sensitivity. I was too stubborn to admit that I had made the wrong decision when I gave up my plans to farm. I had volunteered to join the active SS. The black uniform had become too precious to me and I didn't want to take it off in this way.

Should I become a deserter? As an old-time member of the Nazi Party, I believed in the need for concentration camps. The real "enemies of the state" had to be put away safely; the asocials and the professional criminals who could not be locked up under the prevailing laws had to lose their freedom in order to protect the people from their destructive behavior. I was also firmly convinced that only the SS, the guardians of the new state, could perform this job. But I did not agree with Eicke's views about inmates and his method of enraging the basest feelings of hate among the guard troops. I did not agree with his personnel policy of leaving the prisoners with incompetent people; I did not agree with his practice of unsuitable people in their positions. I was *not* in agreement with the length of sentencing depending on someone's whim. But by staying in the concentration camp, I adopted the views, orders, and decrees which were in force there. Even though I became accustomed to all of the occurrences of the concentration camp, I never became insensitive to human suffering. I always saw it and felt it. But I always had to walk away from it because I was not allowed to be soft. I wanted to have a reputation of being hard. I did not want to be thought of as a weak person.

VII

I went to Sachsenhausen as adjutant [on August 1, 1938]. There I got to learn about concentration camps, their inner workings and practices.

The war came and with it a significant turning point in my life in the concentration camp. On the first day of the war Eicke gave a speech. In that speech he emphasized that now the harsh laws of war had to be obeyed. Every SS soldier had to give his all gully and completely without consideration for his life. Every order had to be considered sacred and even the hardest and most difficult had to be carried out without hesitation. Himmler demanded of each SS officer an exemplary sense of duty and performance for the German people and the nation, even to the point of sacrificing his own life. The main duty of the SS now was to protect Adolf Hitler's nation from all internal dangers during this war. Every enemy of the state who surfaced and everyone who sabotaged the war effort was to be annihilated. The SS had to demonstrate that their stern education was indeed the correct way.

On that very same day the first execution of the war took place at Sachsenhausen. It was a Communist who refused to perform his air raid duties in the Junker aircraft factory in the city of Dessau. At 10:00 p.m., Major General Müller of the Gestapo telephoned and reported that a courier was on the way with an order. This order was to be carried out immediately. Shortly afterwards a car arrived with two State Police officials and a handcuffed civilian. The Commandant broke open the secret order, which stated very briefly, "By order of the Reichs Leader of the SS, John Doe is to be shot. He is to be told this during his arrest and the sentence is to be carried out one hour later." Since I was the adjutant, I was in charge of the headquarters staff. Therefore I had to carry out the execution. I quickly rounded up three older, mature NCOs of the staff, advised them about what had to be done, and lectured them about how they had to conduct themselves. A pole was quickly set into the sand pit of the factory courtyard. The cars arrived immediately. The Commandant told the condemned man to stand at the pole. I led him to it. He calmly prepared himself. I stepped back and gave the order to fire. He collapsed, and I gave him the *coup de grâce* to the head. The doctor examined the body and discovered that three bullets had pierced the heart.

All of the officers present at the execution sat for a while afterwards in the officers' mess. Strangely, no real conversation took place. Everyone was immersed in his own thoughts. Yet all of us were deeply moved by what we had just experienced.

Almost daily I had to report with my execution squad. Most of the cases dealt with saboteurs or those who refused to serve in the army. The reason for the execution was not stated in the execution order, but could only be learned from the Gestapo officer who accompanied the orders.

One case in particular deeply affected me. An SS officer who was also a State Police official with whom I had often worked when he transported important prisoners or delivered important secret documents to the Commandant, was suddenly brought in one night for immediate execution. Just the day before we had sat in the mess hall and talked about the executions. Now the same thing was going to happen to him, and I had to carry out the order. To this day I still cannot understand how I could have calmly given the order to fire. It was a good thing that the three men who did the shooting did not know who he was, for they surely would have trembled. I was so upset I could barely hold the pistol steady when I had to give him the *coup de grâce*. I did manage to pull myself together in such a way that those who were present did not notice anything conspicuous. I confirmed this when I talked with one of the NCOs of the execution squad about this incident a few days later.

So I believed at the time that this kind of harshness was too much for any person to bear. Yet Eicke continuously preached about becoming even harder. An SS soldier had to be able to destroy even his own relatives if they went against the state or the ideas of Adolf Hitler. "There is only one thing that is valid: Orders!" This was Eicke's motto, which appeared at the head of all his letters.

At the beginning of the war prisoners in the concentration camps who were fit for military service were drafted by the draft boards of the various army districts according to their status and either were released to enter the military or were kept in the camps. There were many Jehovah's Witnesses in Sachsenhausen. A large number of them refused to serve in the military and were, therefore, sentenced to death by Himmler as draft dodgers. They were shot to death in the camp in front of the entire assembly of prisoners.

How different each person's approach to death was. The Jehovah's Witnesses were in a way strangely satisfied. One could say they had an almost transfigured mood and had a rock-hard awareness that they were to be allowed to go into Jehovah's kingdom. The draft dodgers and the saboteurs calmly composed and reconciled themselves to the inevitability of the their fate. The professional criminal and the truly asocial appeared to be quite different, either cynical, insolent, or apparently vigorous. Trembling inside with the fear of the great unknown, they raged and fought all the way or whined for a priest to help them.

I will give you two striking examples. The Sass brothers had been arrested in Denmark during a raid and, according to international treaty, were extradited to Germany. These two super criminals had been sentenced to prison, one for twelve years, the other for ten, by a Berlin court after their extradition, which, according to German law, was the maximum sentence they could receive. Two days after the sentencing Himmler, by authority of his special powers, had both of them taken from the holding center and brought to Sachsenhausen for execution by firing squad. They were both to be shot without delay. They were taken by car directly to the sand pit of the industrial courtyard. At the site of the execution, I read the death sentence to them. Immediately they began to yell, "This is impossible. How can you do this? We want to see a priest immediately," and several other things. They absolutely refused to stand at the pole, so I had to have them tied to it. They fought with all their strength against this. I was relieved when I finally gave the order to fire.

A sex offender with several previous arrests had lured an eight-year-old girl into a hallway of a Berlin house. As he was raping her, he strangled her to death. He was sentenced to fifteen years in prison by the court. On that very same day he was brought to Sachsenhausen for execution. Even today I can see him getting out of the car at the entrance to the industrial courtyard. Grinning cynically, he was a depraved-looking older man, a typical asocial. When I read him the death sentence, his face turned a pale yellow. He began to cry, scream, and carry on. Then he cried out for mercy—a disgusting display. I had to have him tied to the pole also. Could it be that these amoral people were in fear of the "great beyond"? I cannot explain their behavior in any other way.

These were only examples that I can remember at this moment, only a small segment of the never-boring life in a concentration camp.

VIII

When Auschwitz was chosen as the site for a concentration camp, the powers that be did not have to look very hard to find a Commandant. So I became the Commandant of the new quarantine camp called Auschwitz. Auschwitz was far off the beaten track in the backwoods of Poland. There the pain-in-the-neck Hoess could indulge his mania for work to his heart's desire—at least, this was Glück's opinion. Under these conditions I began my new assignment.

This assignment was not easy. In the shortest possible time I was supposed to create a transition camp for ten thousand prisoners from the existing complex of well-preserved buildings. The buildings were filthy and teemed with lice, fleas, and other bugs. It is much easier to establish a new camp than it is

49

to take an unsuitable group of buildings and barracks without major remodeling and quickly create a useful concentration camp as I was originally ordered. Before the war, the concentration camps were used to protect Germany from its internal enemies, but because of the war Himmler ordered that their main purpose now was to serve the war effort. Every possible prisoner was to become a defense plant worker; every Commandant was to have his camp absolutely ready for this purpose. According to Himmler's orders Auschwitz was to become a tremendous prisoner defense center. Now all this responsibility fell on my shoulders. From nothing and with nothing, I had to build an enormous enterprise in the quickest possible manner.

Until the beginning of 1942 the main body of prisoners was Polish. They all knew that they would have to remain in the concentration camp at least for the duration of the war. Most of them believed that Germany would lose the war; after Stalingrad practically everyone agreed. By listening to the enemy broadcasts they were accurately informed about Germany's "real situation." It was not very difficult to listen to enemy news since there were enough radios in Auschwitz. We listened to them even in my house. Since according to enemy propaganda the defeat of the Axis powers was only a question of time now, one could say that the Polish prisoners had no reason to despair. There was only one question. Who would be lucky enough to survive the imprisonment?

Anyone on any day could be struck down by diseases to which his physical condition had no more resistance; anyone could suddenly be shot or hanged as a hostage or could unexpectedly be caught up in a resistance movement and thereby brought before Summary Court and sentenced to death. Many of them were tempted to escape from all this misery. There were additional drawbacks to escaping, such as reprisals against the family members and the shooting of ten or more fellow prisoners. Many who escaped cared little about reprisals and took the chance in spite of them. If they had bad luck, then it was all over. Their motto was: Either way you're dead. Their fellow prisoners, their companions in sorrow, had to march by the corpse of the shot escapee so that they could see how an attempt to escape would end. Viewing the body probably frightened many of them to abandon their ideas of escape.

I often wondered what they were thinking as they paraded past the bodies of their dead comrades. If I am able to read faces, I saw the following in them: hardened feelings because of what happened, compassion for the unlucky one, and a desire for revenge and retribution when the time came. I could see the same things in their faces when they were assembled to watch the hangings. The only difference was that at that occasion the fear of suffering the same fate was more noticeable.

I also have to mention here the Summary Court and the killing of hostages. Most of the hostages had been in the camp for quite some time. Neither they nor the camp administration knew they were hostages. Suddenly a telegram would arrive from the Gestapo or from Himmler stating, "The following prisoners are to be shot or hanged as hostages." Compliance with this order had to be reported within a few hours. Those prisoners concerned were taken away from their work areas or pulled out during roll call and brought to the detention block [Block 1]. In the detention block they were informed of the order to execute them. At first, in 1940 and the early part of 1941, they were shot in the back of the neck. The bedridden patients in the hospital infirmary [Block 10] were killed by injection [phenol injection directly into the heart]. The Summary Court in Katowice generally came to Auschwitz every four to six weeks.

The second-largest group, who were supposed to build a POW camp at Birkenau, were the Russian prisoners of war. They came from the army POW camp in Lamsdorf in Upper Silesia and were in a very run-down physical condition. They arrived in Auschwitz after long weeks of marching with very little food supplied to them on route. During the breaks in their march they were simply led into nearby fields and told to "graze" like cattle on everything that was edible.

I was supposed to build the POW camp at Birkenau with these prisoners, who barely had enough energy to stand up. They were perfectly willing to work but were unable to accomplish anything because of their weakened condition. They died like flies because of their weakened physical condition or from the slightest illness, which their bodies could no longer fight off. I saw countless Russians die as they were swallowing turnips and potatoes. The situation really became terrible during the muddy period in the winter of 1941-42. They could bear the cold, but not the dampness and wearing clothes which were always wet. This together with the primitive, half-finished, hastily thrown-together barracks at the start of Camp Birkenau caused the death rate steadily to climb.

Cases of cannibalism happened quite often in Birkenau. Once I found the body of a Russian lying between two piles of bricks. The body had been ripped open with a dull instrument. The liver was missing. They beat each other to death just to get something to eat. They were no longer human. They had become animals who looked for only one thing: food. Of the ten thousand Russian prisoners of war who were supposed to be the main labor force for the construction of the POW camp at Birkenau, only a few hundred were alive by the summer of 1942. This remnant became the elite.

In the summer of 1942, I believe this remnant achieved a mass breakout. A large number were shot in the attempt. Those who were recaptured explained that they ran because of the fear of being gassed, which they expected when the announcement was made that they would be transferred to a newly built section of the camp. There was never any intention to gas these Russians.

The next largest contingent in the camp were the Gypsies. Long before the war the Gypsies were rounded up and put into concentration camps during the campaign against the asocials. One branch of the Federal Criminal Police was solely concerned with the supervision of the Gypsies. Furthermore, the Gypsy camps were continuously checked for biological reasons. Himmler wanted to preserve the two main tribes of Gypsies, the names of which I have forgotten, at all costs. Himmler believed they were direct descendents of Indo-Germanic aborigines and had preserved their customs and culture pure and intact. For research purposes they were all gathered together, accurately registered, and put under state protection as an historical treasure. I can no longer recall how many Gypsies, or those with mixed blood, were in Auschwitz. I only know they completely filled the section of the camp designed for ten thousand prisoners. However, the general conditions were suited for everything but a family camp. The Gypsies able to work were transferred to other camps. By August 1944 there were only about four thousand Gypsies left, and these had to go into the gas chambers. Until that time they did not know what fate was in store for them. Only as they marched barrack after barrack to Crematory I did they figure out what was going on. It was not easy to get them into the gas chamber.

It would have been interesting to observe their lifestyle and their activities, if I didn't know all the horror that lay ahead for them, namely the extermination order. In Auschwitz only the doctors and I knew about this order until the middle of 1944. The doctors had the order from Himmler to separate the sick, especially the children, without making it noticeable. It was the children who had the most trust in the doctors.

IX

How did imprisonment affect the Jews, who were the majority in Auschwitz from 1942 on? How did they behave?

Even in the beginning there were Jews in concentration camps. I knew them very well from my time in Dachau. However, in those days Jews still had the opportunity to leave Germany and go to anywhere in the world that gave them permission to enter. Their stay in the camp was only a question of time or money, and having connections in a foreign country. Many got the necessary visas together within a few weeks and were freed. Only Jews who had violated racial laws, or who were very politically active during the Weimar Republic, had to remain in the camp. The Jews were harassed and persecuted enough as "corrupters of the German people," even by their fellow prisoners.

I have to say something about this. I have always rejected *Der Stürmer*, [Julius] Streicher's anti-Semitic newspaper, because of the disgusting sensationalism calculated to work on man's basest instincts. This newspaper did a lot of damage and has never been of any use to serious scientific anti-Semitism. In fact, it has damaged the cause of anti-Semitism by turning people off. It was no wonder after the collapse of Germany I learned that a Jew edited this newspaper and wrote most of the depraved articles. If you wanted to fight the Jews intellectually, you had to use better weapons than this.

Then came Kristallnacht, instigated by Goebbels in November 1938; throughout all of Germany Jewish businesses were destroyed, or at least all the windows were smashed in retaliation for the killing of von Rath in Paris by a Jew. Everywhere fires broke out in the synagogues and the firemen were deliberately prohibited from fighting the fires. "In order to protect them from the wrath of the German people," all Jews who still played a role in commerce, industry, and business were arrested and brought to the concentration camps as "Jews in protective custody." This is when I first became acquainted with them as a group.

I want to emphasize here that I personally never hated the Jews. I considered them to be the enemy of our nation. However, that was precisely the reason to treat them the same way as the other prisoners. I never made a distinction concerning this. Besides, the feeling of hatred is not in me, but I know what hate is, and how it manifests itself. I have seen it and I have felt it.

The original order of 1941 to annihilate all the Jews stated: "All Jews without exception are to be destroyed." It was later changed by Himmler so that those able to work were to be used in the arms factories. This made Auschwitz the assembly point for the Jews to a degree never before known. The Jews who were imprisoned during the 1930s could still count on the fact that someday they might be released again, which made being in prison psychologically much easier. But for the Jews in Auschwitz, there was no such hope. They knew without exception that they were sentenced to death, and that they would stay alive only as long as they worked. The majority also had no hope or expectation that their sad fate would be changed. They were fatalists. Patiently and apathetically they allowed all the misery, deprivation, and torment to happen to them. The hopelessness of escaping the foreseeable end caused them to become totally withdrawn from what was happening in the camp. This mental breakdown accelerated the physical breakdown. They no longer had the will to live. They had become indifferent to everything and even the slightest physical shock caused them to die. Sooner or later death was certain for them. From what I observed, I firmly maintain that the death rate of most of the Jews was caused not only by the unaccustomed work, or the inadequate food, or the overcrowded living conditions and all the other unpleasantness and poor conditions of the camp, but mainly and most importantly because of their psychological condition. This was even more noticeable among the Jewish women. They collapsed even quicker than the men, even though, from my observation, women generally are much tougher and have more stamina psychologically and physically than do men. When the women had reached the point of no return, they let themselves go completely. They stumbled through the area like ghosts, completely without will, and had to be literally pushed everywhere by others until one day they just quietly died. These walking corpses were a terrible sight.

This applies to the majority of the Jewish prisoners. In many ways the more intelligent ones conducted themselves differently. These were mostly the Jews who were psychologically strong, who had the will to live, and who came mostly from the Western countries. These were the exact ones, especially the doctors, who knew precisely what was going to happen. But they hoped and counted on good luck sparing them. They hoped that somehow or sometime their lives would be saved. They also counted on Germany's collapse because the enemy propaganda reached them easily.

X

According to Himmler's orders, Auschwitz became the largest human killing center in all of history. When he gave me the order personally in the summer of 1941 to prepare a place for mass killings and then carry it out, I could never have imagined the scale, or what the consequences would be. Of course, this order was something extraordinary, something monstrous. However, the reasoning behind the order of this mass annihilation seemed correct to me. At the time I wasted no thoughts about it. I could not allow myself to form an opinion as to whether this mass extermination of the Jews was necessary or not. At the time it was beyond my frame of mind. Since the Führer himself had ordered "The Final Solution of the Jewish Question," there was no second guessing for an old National Socialist, much less an SS officer. "Führer, you order. We obey," was not just a phrase or a slogan.

Since my arrest I have been told repeatedly that I could have refused to obey this order, and even that I could have shot Himmler dead. Something like that was absolutely impossible. Of course, many SS officers moaned and groaned about the many harsh orders. Even then, they carried out every order. As leader of the SS, Himmler's person was sacred. His fundamental orders in the name of the Führer were holy. There was no reflection, no interpretation, no explanation about these orders. Whatever the Führer or Himmler ordered was *always* right.

In the summer of 1941—I am unable to recall the exact date—I was suddenly ordered by Himmler's adjutant to report directly to the Reichsführer SS in Berlin. Contrary to his usual custom, he greeted me with the following: "The Führer has ordered the Final Solution of the Jewish Question. We the SS have to carry out this order. The existing extermination sites in the East are not in a position to carry out these intended operations on a large scale. I have, therefore, chosen Auschwitz for this purpose. First of all, because of the advantageous transport facilities, and secondly, because it allows this area to be easily isolated and disguised. I had first thought of choosing a higher-ranking SS officer for this job so as to avoid any difficulties with someone who doesn't have the competence to carry out such a difficult assignment. You now have to carry out this assignment. It is to remain between the two of us. It is a hard and difficult job which requires your complete commitment, regardless of the difficulties which may arise. You will learn the further details through Major [Adolf] Eichmann of the RSHA [Reich Security Headquarters], who will soon visit you. The administrative departments involved will be notified by me at the appropriate time. You are sworn to the strictest silence regarding this order. Not even your superiors are allowed to know about this. The Jews are the eternal enemies of the German people and must be exterminated. All the Jews within our reach must be annihilated during this war. If we do not succeed in destroying the biological foundation of Jewry now, then one day the Jews will destroy the German people."

After receiving this far-reaching order, I returned to Auschwitz immediately. A short time after that Eichmann came to see me. He revealed the secret plans of the police roundups in the individual countries. I cannot recall the exact sequence anymore. He also mentioned to me the approximate numbers anticipated to be transported, but I don't recall the exact figures. We further discussed how the mass annihilation was to be carried out. Only gas was suitable since killing by shooting the huge numbers expected would be absolutely impossible and would also be a tremendous strain on the SS soldiers who would have to carry out the order as far as women and children were concerned. Eichmann told me about the killings by engine exhaust gas in the gas vans and how they had been used in the East up until now. But this method was not suitable in view of the expected mass transports to Auschwitz. We also discussed killing by carbon monoxide through the showerheads in the shower rooms, but this would also create a problem because too many intricate installations would be needed. The killing of the mentally ill was carried out in various places in Germany using this method. But the production of such great quantities of gas for such large numbers of people would be a problem. We didn't reach any decision about this. We drove around the Auschwitz area to locate a suitable place. We thought the farmhouse at the northwest corner of Birkenau near planned Section III would be suitable. The house had been abandoned, and it was hidden from view by the surrounding trees and bushes and not too far from the railroad. The bodies could be buried in long, deep pits in the nearby meadows. We didn't think about burning them at this time. We calculated that in the space available in the farmhouse [later called Bunker I], approximately eight hundred people could be killed using a suitable gas after the building was made airtight. We later found this to be the actual capacity.

At the end of November there was an official conference in Eichmann's Berlin office about the overall Jewish operation to which I was also invited. Eichmann's deputies reported the status of the police actions in the individual countries and about the difficulties that interfered with the execution of these operations: how those who were arrested were housed, the preparation of the transport trains, scheduling difficulties, and so on. I was not yet able to find out when the operation would begin. Eichmann still had not found a suitable gas.

In the fall of 1941 a special secret order was issued to the POW camps by which the Russian politruks, commissars, and other political functionaries were selected by the Gestapo and moved to the nearest concentration camp to be killed. Small transports of this kind were continuously arriving at Auschwitz. They were shot in the gravel pits at the Monopol Factory or in the courtyard of Block 11. While I was away on camp-related business, Captain Fritzsch, on his own initiative, employed a gas for the killing of three Russian POWs. He crammed the Russians into the individual cells in the basement [of Block 11] and while using gasmasks he threw the Cyclon B gas into the cells, thereby causing their immediate death. The gas called Cyclon B was supplied by the firm of Tesch and Stabenow and was used constantly for insect and rodent control. We always had a large supply of gas canisters available.

When I returned Fritzsch reported to me about how he had used the gas. We used it again to kill the next transport. The gassing was carried out in the basement of Block 11. I viewed the killing wearing a gasmask for protection. Death occurred in the crammed-full cells immediately after the gas was thrown in. Only a brief choking outcry and it was all over. This first gassing of people did not really sink into my mind. Perhaps I was much too impressed by the whole procedure.

I remember well and was much more impressed by the gassing of nine hundred Russians which occurred soon afterwards in the old crematory because the use of Block 11 caused too many problems. The Russians had to undress in the antechamber, then everyone calmly walked into the mortuary because they were told they were to be deloused in there. The entire transport fit exactly in the room. The doors were closed and the gas poured in through the openings in the roof. How long the process lasted, I don't know, but for quite some time sounds could be heard. As the gas was thrown in some of them yelled "Gas!" and a tremendous screaming and shoving started toward both doors, but the doors were able to withstand all the force.

It was not until several hours later that the doors were opened and the room aired out. There for the first time I saw the gassed bodies in mass. But I must admit openly that the gassings had a calming effect on me, since in the near future the mass annihilation of the Jews was to begin. Up to this point it was not clear to me, nor to Eichmann, how the killing of the expected masses was to be done. Perhaps by gas? But how, and what kind of gas? Now we had discovered the gas and the procedure.

I was always horrified by the death by firing squads, especially when I thought of the huge numbers of women and children who would have to be killed. I had had enough of hostage executions, and the mass killings by firing squad ordered by Himmler and Heydrich. Now I was at ease. We were all saved from these bloodbaths, and the victims would be spared until the last moment. That is what I worried about the most when I thought of

Eichmann's accounts of the mowing down of the Jews with machine guns and pistols by the Einsatzgruppe. Horrible scenes were supposed to have occurred: people running away even after being shot, the killing of those who were only wounded, especially the women and children. Another thing on my mind was the many suicides among the ranks of the SS Special Action Squads who could no longer mentally endure wading in the bloodbath. Some of them went mad.

During Eichmann's next visit I reported all this to him, about how the Cyclon B was used, and we decided that for the future mass annihilations we would use this gas.

XI

I am unable to recall when the destruction of the Jews began—probably in September 1941, or perhaps not until January 1942. At first we dealt with the Jews from Upper Silesia. These Jews were arrested by the Gestapo from Katowice and transported via the Auschwitz-Dziediez railroad and unloaded there. As far as I can recall, these transports never numbered more than a thousand persons.

A detachment of SS from the camp took charge of them at the railroad ramp, and the officer in charge marched them to the bunker [I] in two groups. This is what we called the extermination installation. Their luggage remained on the ramp and was later brought between the DAW [German Armaments Works] and the railroad station. The Jews had to undress at the bunker and were told that they would have to go into the delousing rooms. All of the rooms—there were five of them—were filled at the same time. The air-tight doors were screwed tight, and the contents of the gas crystal canisters emptied into the rooms through special hatches.

After half an hour the doors were opened and the bodies were pulled out. Each room had two doors. They were then moved using small carts on special tracks to the ditches. The clothing was brought by trucks to the sorting place. All of the work was done by a special contingent of Jews [the Sonderkommando]. They had to help those who were about to die with the undressing, the filling up of the bunkers, the clearing of the bunkers, removal of bodies, as well as digging the mass graves and, finally, covering the graves with earth. These Jews were housed separately from the other prisoners and, according to Eichmann's orders, they themselves were to be killed after each large extermination action.

After the first transports Eichmann brought an order from Himmler, which specified that the gold teeth were to be pulled from the mouths of the bodies, and the hair was to be cut from the dead women. This work was also carried out by special groups of Jews. The gold taken from the teeth was melted into bars by the dentists in the SS hospital and sent monthly to the Sanitary Office Headquarters. The hair cut from the women prisoners was sent to a firm in Bavaria to be used for the war effort.

Supervising the extermination at that time was the camp commander [Captain Hans Aumeier] or the duty officer [Master Sergeant Gerhard Palitzsch]. The sick who could not be brought to the gassing rooms were simply killed with small-caliber weapons by shooting them in the back of the neck. An SS doctor also had to be present. The gas was administered by trained medics.

During the spring of 1942 we were still dealing with small police actions. But during the summer the transports became more numerous and we were forced to build another extermination site. The farm area west of Crematories IV and V, which were built later, was chosen and prepared. Five barracks were built, two near Bunker I and three near Bunker II. Bunker II was the larger one. It held about 1,200 people.

As late as the summer of 1942 the bodies were still buried in mass graves. Not until the end of the summer of 1942 did we start burning them. At first we put two thousand bodies on a large pile of wood. Then we opened up the mass graves and burned the new bodies on top of the old ones from the earlier burials. At first we poured waste oil over the bodies. Later on we used methanol. The burning went on continuously—all day and all night. By the end of November all the mass graves were cleared. The number of buried bodies in the mass graves was 107,000. This number contains not only the first Jewish transports which were gassed when we started the burnings, but also the bodies of the prisoners who died in the main Auschwitz camp during the winter of 1941–42 because the crematory was out of order. The prisoners who died at Birkenau [Auschwitz II] are included in that number.

During his visit in the summer of 1942, Himmler very carefully observed the entire process of annihilation. At that time there were no open-pit burnings. He did not complain about anything, but he didn't say anything about it either. Shortly after Himmler's visit, SS Colonel Blobel from Eichmann's office arrived and brought Himmler's order, which stated that all mass graves were to be opened and all the bodies cremated. It further stated that all the ashes were to be disposed of in such a way that later on there would be no way to determine the number of those cremated.

XII

Originally, all the Jews transported to Auschwitz by the authority of Eichmann's office were to be destroyed without exception, according to Himmler's orders. This also applied to the Jews from Upper Silesia. But during the arrival of the first transports of German Jews, the order was given that all able-bodied men and women were to be separated and put to work in the arms factories. This occurred before the construction of the women's camp, since the need for a women's camp in Auschwitz only arose as a result of this order.

The selection of able-bodied Jews was supposed to be made by SS doctors. I believed that only strong and healthy Jews should be selected to work. The sorting process went as follows: The railway cars were unloaded one after another. After depositing their baggage, the Jews had to individually pass in front of an SS doctor, who decided on their physical fitness as they marched past him. Those who were considered able-bodied were immediately escorted into the camp in small groups. On average in all transports between 25 and 30 percent were found fit for work, but this figure fluctuated considerably. Jewish doctors and administrative personnel were taken into the camp without exception.

It became apparent during the first cremations in the open air that in the long run it would not be possible to continue in that manner. During bad weather or when a strong wind was blowing, the stench of burning flesh was carried for many miles and caused the entire area to talk about the burning of Jews. The anti-aircraft defenses protested against the fires because they could be seen from great distances at night. Nevertheless, the burnings had to continue, even at night, unless further transports were to be refused. It was for these reasons that the energetic planning and construction of the two large crematories [II and III] and the building of the two smaller crematories [IV and V] were completed in 1943.

The two large crematories were built in the winter of 1942–43 and brought into service in the spring of 1943. Each had five ovens with three doors [retorts] per oven and could cremate about two thousand bodies in less than twenty-four hours. Technical difficulties made it impossible to increase the capacity. Crematories [II and III] both had underground undressing rooms and underground gas chambers in which the air could be completely ventilated. The bodies were taken to the ovens on the floor above by an elevator. The [two] gas chambers could hold three thousand people, but this number was never achieved, since the individual transports were never that large.

The two smaller crematories [IV and V] were capable of burning about 1,500 bodies in twenty-four hours, according to the calculations made by the construction company called Topf of Erfurt. It soon became apparent, however, that the poor construction of these two ovens, each with four retorts, did not meet the requirements. Crematory [IV] failed completely after a short time and later was not used at all. Crematory [V] had to be repeatedly shut down, since after its fires had been burning for four to six weeks the ovens or the chimneys burned out.

The provisional building [the red farmhouse] was demolished when work began on building section [B] III in Birkenau. [Gas Chamber] II [the white farmhouse], later designated Bunker V, was used up until the last and was also kept as a standby when breakdowns occurred in Crematories [II or III]. When larger numbers of transports were received, the gassing was carried out by day in Crematory V, while Crematories I to IV were used for the transports that arrived during the night. There was no limit to the number of bodies that could be burned at [the white farmhouse] as long as the cremations could be carried out both day and night. Because of enemy air raids, no further cremations were allowed during the night after 1944. The highest total figure of people gassed and cremated in twenty-four hours was slightly more than nine thousand. This figure was reached in the summer of 1944, during the action in Hungary, using all the installations except Crematory [IV]. On that day five trains arrived because of delays on the rail lines, instead of three, as was expected, and in addition the railroad cars were more crowded than usual.

During my earlier interrogations I gave the number of 2.5 million Jews who arrived at Auschwitz to be exterminated. This figure was given to me by Eichmann. I myself never knew the total number, and I have nothing to help me arrive at an estimate. I regard a total of 2.5 million as far too high. Even Auschwitz had limits to its destructive capabilities. Figures given by former prisoners are figments of their imagination and have no foundation in fact.

XIII

The extermination process in Auschwitz took place as follows: Jews selected for gassing were taken as quietly as possible to the crematories. The men were already separated from the women. In the undressing chamber, prisoners of the Sonderkommandos, who were specially chosen for this purpose, would tell them in their own language that they were going to be bathed and deloused, and that they must leave their clothing neatly together, and, above all, remember where they put them, so that they would be able to find them again quickly after the delousing. The Sonderkommando had the greatest interest in seeing that the operation proceeded smoothly and quickly. After undressing, the Jews went into the gas chamber, which was furnished with showers and water pipes and gave a realistic impression of a bathhouse. The women went in first with their children, followed by the men who were always fewer in number. This part of the operation nearly always went smoothly since the Sonderkommando would always calm those who showed any anxiety or perhaps even had some clue as to their fate. As an additional precaution, the Sonderkommando and an SS soldier always stayed in the chamber until the very last moment.

The door would be screwed shut and the waiting disinfection squads would immediately pour the gas [crystals] into the vents in the ceiling of the gas chamber down an air-shaft which went to the floor. This ensured the rapid distribution of the gas. The process could be observed through the peephole in the door. Those who were standing next to the airshaft were killed immediately. I can state that about one-third died immediately. The remainder staggered about and began to scream and struggle for air. The screaming, however, soon changed to gasping and in a few moments everyone lay still. After twenty minutes at most no movement could be detected.

The door was opened a half an hour after the gas was thrown in and the ventilation system was turned on. Work was immediately started to remove the corpses. There was no noticeable change in the bodies and no signs of convulsions or discoloration. Only after the bodies had been left lying for some time— several hours—did the usual death stains appear where they were laid. Seldom did it occur that they were soiled with feces. There were no wounds of any kind. The faces were not contorted.

The Sonderkommando now set about removing the gold teeth and cutting the hair from the women. After this, the bodies were taken up by an elevator and laid in front of the ovens, which had meanwhile been fired up. Depending on the size of the bodies, up to three corpses could be put in through one oven door at the same time. The time required for cremation also depended on the number of bodies in each retort, but on average it took twenty minutes.

During the period when the fires were kept continuously burning without a break, the ashes fell through the grates and were constantly removed and crushed to powder. The ashes were taken by trucks to the Vistula [River], where they immediately dissolved and drifted away.

XIV

Never did I see or ever hear even a syllable breathed to those who were going to be gassed as to what their fate was. On the contrary, they tried everything to fool them. Most of all, they tried to calm those who seemed to guess what was ahead.

The women tried to hide the babies because they thought the disinfection process would harm their infants. The little children cried mostly because of the unusual setting in which they were being undressed. But after their mothers or the Sonderkommando encouraged them, they calmed down and continued playing, teasing each other, clutching a toy as they went into the gas chamber. I also watched how some women who suspected or knew what was happening, even with the fear of death all over their faces, still managed enough strength to play with their children and to talk to them lovingly. There were many heartbreaking scenes like this which affected all who were present. In the spring of 1942 hundreds of people in the full bloom of life walked beneath the budding fruit trees of the farm into the gas chamber to their death, most of them without a hint of what was going to happen to them. To this day I can still see these pictures of the arrivals, the selections, and the procession to their death.

As the selection process continued at the unloading ramps, there were an increasing number of incidences. Tearing apart families, separating the men from the women and the children, caused great unrest and excitement in the entire transport. Separating those who were able to work only increased the seriousness of the situation. No matter what, the families wanted to stay together. So it happened that even those selected to work ran back to the other members of their family, or the mothers with their children tried to get back to their husbands, or to the older children.

Oftentimes order was restored by sheer

force. The Jews have a very strong sense of family. They cling to each other like leeches, but from what I observed, they lack a feeling of solidarity. I heard about, and also experience, Jews who gave the addresses of fellow Jews who were in hiding. These Jews in particular came from Western Europe. I cannot explain what motivated them to do this. Was it personal revenge, or were they jealous because they did not want the others to live on?

As strange as that was, so was the general behavior of the Sonderkommando. All of them knew with certainty that when it was over, they themselves would suffer the same fate as thousands of their race had before them, in whose destruction they were very helpful. In spite of this they still did their job with an eagerness and in a caring, helpful way during the undressing, yet they would also use force with those who resisted undressing. This always amazed me. They never spoke to the victims about what was ahead of them. They also led away the troublemakers and then held on to them firmly while they were being shot. They led these victims in such a way that they could not see the NCO who stood ready with his gun. This enabled him to aim at the back of their necks without being noticed. It was the same when they dealt with the sickly and feeble who could not be brought into the gas chambers. All this was done in a matter-of-fact manner, as if they themselves were the exterminators. They dragged the bodies from the gas chambers, removed the gold teeth, cut off the hair, then dragged the bodies to the pits or to the ovens. On top of that, they had to maintain the fires in the pits, pour off the accumulated fat, and poke holes into the burning mountains of bodies, so that more oxygen could enter. All these jobs they performed with an indifferent coolness, just as if this was an everyday affair. Where did the Jews of the Sonderkommando get the strength to perform this horrible job day and night?

I really have watched this closely, but could never get to the bottom of their behavior. The way the Jews lived and died was a puzzle I could not solve. I could relate countless more of these experiences and occurrences of the type I have described so far. These are only excerpts from the total process of the annihilation. They are only glimpses.

XV

Hour upon hour I had to witness all that happened. I had to watch day and night, whether it was the dragging and burning of the bodies, the teeth being ripped out, the cutting of the hair; I had to watch all this horror. For hours I had to stand in the horrible, haunting stench while the mass graves were dug open, and the bodies were dragged out and burned. I also had to watch the process of death itself through the peephole of the gas chamber because the doctors called my attention to it. I had to do all of this because I was the one to whom everyone looked, and because I had to show everybody that I was not only the one who gave the orders and issued the directives, but that I was also willing to be present at whatever task I ordered my men to perform.

When something upset me very much and it was impossible for me to go home to my family, I would climb onto my horse and ride until I chased the horrible pictures away. I often went into the horse stables during the night, and there found peace among my darlings. Often at home my mind would suddenly recall some incident at the killing sites. That's when I had to get out because I couldn't stand being in the loving surroundings of my family. When I watched our children happily at play, or saw my wife bubbling with happiness over the baby, this thought often came to me: How long will your happiness continue? My wife never understood my troubled moods and merely blamed them on the problems connected with my work. Many a night as I stood out there on the railroad platforms, at the gas chambers, or at the burnings, I was forced to think of my wife and children. When one watches women enter the gas chambers with their children, one's thoughts naturally turn to one's own family. I was no longer happy at Auschwitz once the mass annihilation began. I became dissatisfied with myself.

And yet, everyone at Auschwitz believed

the Commandant really had the good life. Yes, my family had it good in Auschwitz, every wish that my wife or my children had was fulfilled. The children could live free and easy. My wife had her flower paradise. The prisoners tried to give my wife every consideration and tried to do something nice for the children. By the same token no former prisoner can say that he was treated poorly in any way in our house. My wife would have loved to give a present to every prisoner who performed a service for us. The children constantly begged me for cigarettes for the prisoners. The children especially loved the gardeners. In our entire family there was a deep love for farming and especially for animals. Every Sunday I had to drive them across all the fields, walk them through the stables, and we could never skip visiting the dog kennels. Their greatest love was for our two horses and our colt. The prisoners who worked in the household were always dragging in some animal the children kept in the garden. Turtles, martens, cats, or lizards; there was always something new and interesting in the garden. The children splashed around in the summertime in the small pool in the garden or in the Sola River. Their greatest pleasure was when Daddy went into the water with them.

Today I deeply regret that I didn't spend more time with my family. My wife often urged me, "Don't always think of your duty, think of your family too." But what did my wife know about the things that depressed me? She never found out.

XVI

What do I think of the Third Reich today? What is my opinion of Himmler? The SS? The concentration camps? And the Security Police? How do I now see all the events I have experienced?

I am now as I was then, as far as my philosophy of life is concerned. I am still a National Socialist. A person who has believed in an ideology, a philosophy, for almost twenty-five years and who was bound up in it body and soul cannot simply throw it away just because the embodiment of that idea, the National Socialist state and its leaders, acted wrongly. In fact, criminally and through their failure our world collapsed and the entire German people have been plunged into unspeakable misery for decades into the future. I cannot do that.

Today I realize that the extermination of the Jews was wrong, absolutely wrong. It was exactly because of this mass extermination that Germany earned itself the hatred of the entire world. The cause of anti-Semitism was not served by this act at all, in fact, just the opposite. The Jews have come much closer to their final goal.

How could it come to the atrocities in the concentration camps? I have already explained enough in these pages. Now, when I have to hear the descriptions of the horrible tortures that took place in Auschwitz and in other camps, I get cold shudders. It is true—I knew that Auschwitz prisoners had been mistreated by the SS, by the civilian employees, and not in the least by their own fellow prisoners. I used every means at my disposal, but I was unable to stop it. One person is no match for such viciousness, depravity, and cruelty.

Yes, I was hard and strict. As I see it today, often too hard and too strict. Yes, I said many a bad word in anger over the deplorable conditions, or the carelessness, and said many things which I never should have done. But I was never cruel, nor did I let myself get carried away to the point of mistreating prisoners. A great deal happened in Auschwitz, presumably in my name, on my direction, on my orders, about which I neither knew, nor would have tolerated, nor approved of. However, all this did take place in Auschwitz, and I am responsible for it because according to camp regulations: The camp Commandant is *fully responsible* for everything that happens in his camp.

I am now at the end of my life. Everything of importance which I experienced in my life, all the events which influenced me strongly, which touched me in some special way, I have laid down in these notes according to the truth and the reality as I saw it, and the way I experienced it. My tremendous love for my country and my feeling for everything German brought me into the NSDAP [the Nazi party] and into the SS. I believed that the National Socialist world philosophy was the only one that suited the German people. The SS was, in my opinion, the most energetic defender of this philosophy, and the only one capable of leading the German people back to a life more in keeping with its character. My family was the second thing that was sacred to me. I am firmly anchored to it. Worrying about their future is always uppermost in my mind. The farm was supposed to be our homestead. My wife and I saw in the children our purpose in life. It was to be our life's task to enable them to get a good education and create a stable home life for them. And that's why now most of my thoughts deal mainly with only my family. What will become of them? As far as I am concerned, I have written myself off. I do not worry about this anymore. I am finished with it. But my wife, my children?

Fate has played strange tricks on me. How many times did I miss death by a hair: in the last war, in the Free Corps battles, during work-related accidents, the car accident in 1941 on the Autobahn; then in 1942 I had a riding accident in which a heavy stallion crashed down onto me; and again during air raids. So often I wouldn't have bet a dime on my chances, and yet I came through it all. Also, in the car accident just before the evacuation of Ravensbrück. Everyone thought I was dead; the way things looked I couldn't possibly still be alive. Then the vial of poison broke before I was arrested. Everywhere fate has spared me from death only to do away with me now in such a shameful manner. How I envy my comrades who were allowed to die an honest soldier's death. Without realizing it, I became a cog in the wheel of the huge extermination machine of the Third Reich. The machine is smashed, the motor has perished, and I must perish with it. The world demands it.

May the general public simply go on seeing me as the bloodthirsty beast, the cruel sadist, the murderer of millions, because the broad masses cannot conceive the Commandant of Auschwitz in any other way. They would never be able to understand that he also had a heart and that he was not evil.

AFTERWORD

Ian Buruma

In her book *Eichmann in Jerusalem*, Hannah
Arendt ascribed the capacity of ordinary
human beings to commit evil acts, such as
consigning millions of people to their deaths
by the stroke of a pen, to a catastrophic lack
of imagination. She never implied that such
acts of evil are banal, just that the people who
commit them, as it were without thinking, can
be. Whether Adolf Eichmann, who had mur-
derous fantasies about killing every last Jew,
could truly be described as ordinary is perhaps
open to question. One of his chief henchman,
a man who actually carried out the dirty
work, the Auschwitz commandant Rudolf
Hoess, might come closer to her idea of the
banal killer.

Hoess, the son of an authoritarian "fanatically Catholic" father, was mediocre in every way except for his capacity for work, which, in his case, meant mass murder. He was a tireless worker, fanatical not about his childhood faith (his parents wanted him to become a priest), but about order, following the rules, doing everything by the book, making sure there were no loose ends, running a tight ship, and so forth. He wrote an account of his wartime career, while waiting for his sentence in a Polish prison in 1946, at the instigation of a Polish psychologist and the prosecuting attorney. In this clumsily written memoir, he insisted that he was never a cruel man. He always treated the slave workers in his Auschwitz home correctly. Certainly—order must prevail—he gave the prisoners no quarter; he was harsh, "perhaps sometimes too harsh," but he never tormented a prisoner without reason. He was not a sadist, he insists. Physical punishment, such as flogging, he found distasteful. Guards who tortured prisoners for their pleasure were, in his considered view, deplorable.

Although Hoess recognized that bad mistakes had been made in the name of Nazism, he remained convinced that National Socialism was the right creed for Germany. Mass extermination of the Jews, he declared, had been the wrong way to go about things, if only because it harmed the cause of "serious anti-Semitism." Quite what he meant by serious anti-Semitism is not spelled out, but then Hoess was not a reflective man.

He is more forthcoming on the practical details of his job. In theory, for example, the three crematories, manufactured by the Topf concern of Erfurt, were capable of burning two thousand corpses every twenty-four hours. In fact, it proved to be impossible for "fire-technical reasons" to burn more than fifteen hundred corpses in twenty-four hours. Before Zyklon-B, originally devised to exterminate vermin, could be employed, much to Hoess's "relief" by the way, he worried that carbon monoxide couldn't do the job efficiently. It involved building too many new facilities. The material was lacking. Mass shooting, too, was problematic, because it was too hard on the killers. No, Zyklon-B was an excellent solution, better for the Germans, but also better for the Jews, for "we would all be spared from bloodbaths." The curious use of "we" implies that Germans and Jews were all in this together, and the Nazis killed with kindness.

This could only have been written by a man without any imagination whatsoever, or at least any moral imagination. Empathy, according to Hoess's own account, was never his strong point. Hoess never witnessed an instance of tenderness between his parents, nor did he feel any tenderness for his siblings. His only deep feelings during his childhood were reserved for Hans, a black pony. And although Hoess found a kind of home in "the comradeship of his comrades" in the SS, he seems to have had no close friends.

If he had any feelings left by the time he began his career in Nazi concentration camps, first in Dachau, and then Sachsenhausen, before becoming commandant in Auschwitz, he had learned how to suppress them. Hoess explains his fear of looking weak in the eyes of his comrades. To the outside world, he was the hard man, stony-faced at all times, ready to carry out his orders, whatever they were, to the best of his abilities, without a trace of emotion. Hoess was Heinrich Himmler's ideal SS man. Killing without feeling was seen as a form of heroic self-sacrifice.

Yet to say that he was entirely without private feeling would be an error. For he felt sorry for himself. His wife told him not to work so hard and to spend more time with his family. But Hoess, as he frequently assures the reader, was incapable of forsaking his duty. The German nation demanded self-sacrifice, and this filled him with pride, but also with moments of melancholy. The job of mass murder had to be completed. The führer wanted it, Himmler had ordered it, and an order, for a good SS officer, was sacrosanct. But it was no fun. "Since the mass extermination began," Hoess declares, "I was no longer happy at Auschwitz."

The account of Rudolf Hoess has been published in many languages, under many titles, some more lurid than others. The prose is wooden and strangely bloodless, like the field notes of an engineer, writing about the nuts and bolts of constructing a sewage plant. The tone veers from technical explanation, to absurd romanticism about the German spirit and the soldierly life, to repulsive self-pity. This is not the kind of thing that lends itself to drama or any artistic enterprise. Yet that is what Jürg Amann, a Swiss playwright, has tried to distill from Hoess's writings. His edited version is meant to be read not just in book form, but declaimed in a theater or on radio.

The task is daunting. How can one dramatize a criminal lack of imagination, through the lifeless words of a man who can express no emotion besides self-pity? Amann has not rewritten Hoess. Nothing was added. He does not appear to approve of fictionalizing Nazi genocide. In fact, he calls that "obscene." Reality is what he is after: in this case, the reality of Rudolf Hoess, the consummate professional of the Holocaust.

Since the text is primarily aimed at a German audience, Amann can take a great deal of knowledge for granted, and yet it is perhaps an even trickier thing to pull off in Germany than elsewhere. Nazi texts, such as Hitler's *Mein Kampf*, are still banned, as is the use of Nazi symbols, or indeed theories that deny the Holocaust. Hoess does not deny that Jews were systematically murdered, or that he played an active role in the genocide himself. This alone makes his account, though soaked in Nazi propaganda, a very important document, not just in Germany, but everywhere, especially since there are still people who feel the need to deny that there was such a thing as the Holocaust.

Amann's method is to pare the original text down to its bare essentials, stripped of all wordy evasions and self-serving rhetoric. This does not mean that everything Hoess says in the minimalist, edited version of his account is necessarily true. He lies about his wife, for example. Mrs. Hoess and the children, Hoess writes, were sacred to him, almost as sacred as the German nation. And so he feels bad when his wife tells him to think less about his duty and more about his family. But he says, "How could my wife know about the things that oppressed me? She never had any idea." When asked about his conjugal relations, however, he later admitted that his wife would no longer have sex with him after she became aware of the precise nature of his work.

Even the things he holds to be sacred, such as his family or the glories of the Third Reich, are described without human feeling. They comes across as abstractions, as overblown rhetoric, sentimental in the literal sense of the word: displaced emotion. The reader senses that he expresses certain pious feelings because he feels that it behooves an SS man to have them; they, too, are part of his duty, of the order of things: *Heimat*, family, *Reich*.

In a sense, Hoess was probably right about himself. He was not a sadist, or a monster, who acted out of malice. That would be to invest what he did with too much emotion. He may even be telling the truth, when he claims never to have hated the Jews (unlike Eichmann, for example, or Hitler himself, both of whom made their loathing quite clear). Hatred has no place in his ruthlessly circumscribed world; it might make a mess. To be sure, he shared the sentimental, and brutal, Nazi vision of a Germanic, pure-race utopia, peopled by warriors, farmers, and fertile Teutonic mothers. Jews had to be eliminated; of that he was convinced. And he never doubted that Hitler was always right. But if Hoess had been told to murder all brunettes, as enemies of his people, he would have set himself to that task with equal zeal. Hoess is the utterly hollow man. For him it isn't just a matter of *Befehl ist Befehl* (orders must be obeyed). No, orders are everything. Without orders, the hollow man would be helpless, adrift in terrifying nothingness.

So the minimalist version of *The Commandant* conveys the inhumanity of Hoess most effectively. It has the right tone of utter bleakness, devoid of anything that makes life worth living. He was not just a mediocre everyman. The commander of Auschwitz was so banal, so obsessed with his task at hand, that he could not even imagine that murdering millions of innocent men, women, and children was a monstrous thing to do. Duty called. The problems were vast. They took him away from his family. This made him unhappy.

ABOUT THE EDITOR

Born in 1947, Jürg Amann studied German literature in Zurich and Berlin and wrote his dissertation on Franz Kafka. Since 1976, he has been a prolific freelance writer of plays, essays and literary criticism. He has received numerous awards for his work, including the Ingeborg Bachmann Prize, the Conrad Ferdinand Meyer Prize, and the Schiller Prize. He lives in Switzerland.